INTRODUCTORY NOTE FOR PARENTS, FAMILY, FRIENDS AND CARERS.

Reflect on the advantages of encouraging your children to explore these activities.

Engaging with nature, whether through outdoor activities or simply spending time in natural surroundings, has been shown to positively impact mental health and wellbeing. Interacting with nature has a calming effect, reducing stress levels and promoting relaxation.

Gazing into the night sky can evoke feelings of wonder and awe, fostering a sense of perspective and connectedness to something larger than oneself

Playing with friends or engaging in social activities strengthens social bonds and provides emotional support, which is crucial for mental wellbeing.

Creating art, whether through painting, drawing, writing, or other forms of artistic expression, allows individuals to process emotions, enhance self-awareness, and find joy in creativity. Being content with what one has and practicing gratitude fosters a positive mindset and reduces feelings of discontentment or jealousy.

Singing and music can uplift mood, reduce anxiety, and provide a means of self-expression. Singing releases endorphins, serotonin and dopamine, the 'happy' chemicals that boost your mood and make you feel good about yourself.

Acts of kindness and caring for others not only benefit the recipients but also enhance one's own sense of purpose, belonging, and self-worth.

Meditation practices such as, reflecting, having 'quiet time' and mindfulness meditation, improve emotional regulation, reduce stress and anxiety, and promote overall mental clarity and resilience.

Together, these activities and practices contribute to a holistic approach to mental health, nurturing emotional wellbeing and enhancing the quality of life of children, adolescents and adults.

Sometimes we have funny feelings inside that don't feel right. We can feel sad, angry, frightened, confused, and we are not sure how to fix it.

It's like doing a jigsaw puzzle, but we are not quite sure how to solve it. We can always find a piece of the puzzle that fits just right for you!

Sometimes I want to cry...

... then I stop to smell a beautiful flower and it smells so good.

Sometimes I am scared...

... then I look at the stars, and see them twinkling in the night, and I don't feel like I'm on my own.

Sometimes I am angry...

... then I play games with my friends,
and we laugh and talk and hug, and I feel better.

Sometimes I feel sad...

... then I draw a pretty picture
and wonder where such a place could be.

Sometimes I feel I want what other kids have...

... then I think of things that I have and love, and that makes me feel happy.

Sometimes I feel alone...

... then I hear nice music and start to sing.

Sometimes I don't feel special...

... then I say something nice to someone,
and it makes them and me smile.

Sometimes I do things that are naughty...

... then I want to care more
and try to be good more of the time.

Sometimes I am too busy...

... then I think about nothing
and I enjoy being in the moment.

Then I feel really good!
Just like when the puzzle is all finished.

So... there can always be a way to solve the puzzles!

Why don't you write down some things that make you feel good and list the people you can help you?

Then you can do those things and get help from those people when the puzzle pieces don't fit.